Ella and the Toy Rabbit

Story by Dawn McMillan

Illustrations by Pat Reynolds

Ella and Grandma went into the toy shop.

3

"Look at the toys!" said Ella.
"I like this tiger,
and I like this horse!"

4

Grandma went to look
at the puzzles.

Ella ran to look
at the toy rabbits.

"I like this blue rabbit,"
said Ella.
"Look at it, Grandma."

"**Grandma**!" she cried.
"I can not see you!"

Ella ran to look for Grandma.

"Grandma!" she cried.

"Where are you?"

"I'm here, Ella!" said Grandma.

"I went to look at the rabbits," cried Ella.

"And you went away."

Grandma and Ella went back to see the toy rabbits.

"Look at this rabbit," said Grandma.

15

"I love this blue rabbit,"
said Ella.